Leo

THIS BOOK BELONGS TO:

_____

# THE WONDERFUL WORLD OF ZODIACS

## LEO

Mimi Jones

Dedicated to the knowledge seekers.

All rights reserved.
No part of this book may be reproduced in any form or by any means, electronic or mechanical, and no photocopying or recording, unless you have written permission from the author.

ISBN 978-1-958985-50-2

Text copyright © 2025 by Mimi Jones

www.joeysavestheday.com

A Mimi Book

## Dates:

Leo spans from July 23 to August 22.

# Ruling Planet:

The Sun rules Leo.

## Symbol:

The Lion represents Leo.

# STUBBORN

## Weakness:
Leos can be stubborn and crave attention.

## Color:

Their lucky colors are gold, orange, and red.

## Lucky Numbers:

1, 3, 10, and 19 are lucky for Leos.

## Compatibility:

Leo gets along well with Aries, Sagittarius, Gemini, and Libra.

### ARIES

### SAGITTARIUS

### GEMINI

### LIBRA

## Dislikes:

They dislike being ignored and dull routines.

*Leo*

## Likes:

Leos love creativity, admiration, and being in the spotlight.

## Career:

They excel in careers that allow them to shine and lead.

## Positive Trait:

Leos are very generous and warm-hearted.

# Negative Trait:

Sometimes, they can be a bit too self-centered.

## Motto:

Their motto is "I will."

## Favorite Day:

Sunday is their favorite day.

SUNDAY

## Health:

Leos should take care of their heart and spine.

## Hobbies:

They enjoy performing, entertaining, and artistic pursuits.

## Style:

They prefer bold, glamorous, and regal styles.

## Challenges:

Leos need to learn to balance humility with their natural confidence.

# Friendship:

They are loyal friends who will fiercely protect and uplift you.

## Influence:

They inspire others with their courage and enthusiasm.

# LEO

## Favorite Activities:

Leos love activities that let them express themselves and take center stage.

"BE *yourself*"

## Birthstones:

### Ruby and peridot.

If this Zodiac gem tickled your celestial fancy, then you're in for a treat! Dive into my other Zodiac delights right here:

www.mimibooks.com

**THE END!**